# UP CLOSE!

## Exploring Nature
### with a Magnifying Glass

Written by Sarah Jane Brian
Illustrated by Dick Twinney and John Barber

Reader's Digest Children's Books™
Pleasantville, New York • Montréal, Québec

READER'S DIGEST CHILDREN'S BOOKS
Reader's Digest Road
Pleasantville, NY 10570-7000

*Consultant: John McLeran, Director, Woodcock Nature Center, Wilton, Connecticut*

Manufactured in China.
10 9 8 7 6 5 4 3 2


Library of Congress Cataloging-in-Publication Data

Brian, Sarah Jane.
    Up close! : exploring nature with a magnifying glass / written by Sarah Jane Brian ; illustrated by Dick Twinney and John Barber.
        p. cm. — (Reader's Digest explorer guides)
    ISBN 1-57584-965-8 (paperback)
    1. Nature study—Juvenile literature. 2. Magnifying glasses—Juvenile literature. [1. Nature study. Magnifying glasses.] I. Twinney, Dick, ill. II. Barber, John, ill. III. Title. IV. Series.

QH51 .B67 2001                         508—dc21                         00-042539

A NOTE TO READERS AND PARENTS

This publication contains the opinions and ideas of its author and is designed to provide useful information to the reader on the subject matter covered. When engaging in any activities that may be suggested in or relate to the subject of this publication, always exercise caution, and children should always be under adult supervision. Any references in this publication to any products or services do not constitute or imply an endorsement or recommendation. The publisher and the author specifically disclaim any responsibility for any liability, loss, or risk (personal, financial, or otherwise) which may be claimed or incurred as a consequence, directly or indirectly, of the use and/or application of any of the contents of this publication.

# Contents

# Get Close to Nature!

Natural wonders are all around you. You'll find them in parks, in the woods, on the beach—even in your own backyard. But how often do you look at them up close? Try looking at a dandelion or a mushroom, an ant or a slug, with your magnifying glass. You may be surprised at what you see.

The trick is knowing how to look and what to look for. That's where *Up Close!* can help. You'll discover some amazing animals and plants, and learn the secrets of those you've seen many times before. You'll find out what to look for in different places, or habitats, where animals and plants live. And you can even use your magnifying glass in this book—to look for creatures hidden in different scenes. Then take a walk and see if you can find them outside.

# Are You Ready?

Before you head for the great outdoors, make sure you're prepared. If you're exploring anywhere but your backyard, don't go alone. Take an adult and a friend along. Tell someone where you're going and when you'll be back. Ask permission before you go on private property.

Wear sturdy shoes or waterproof boots if it's wet or muddy outside. If it's chilly, wear layers. You can always take off

- Look before reaching under rocks or into holes—you never know what may be hiding inside.
- Don't eat wild berries—they may be poisonous.
- Don't touch wild animals—they may bite.

your jacket or sweater if you get too warm. Make sure whatever you wear is okay to get dirty.

Take a watch to keep track of time. Carry water and a snack. Dried fruit and nuts are good foods when you're on the move. Remember to put on sunblock and bug spray.

Take along some small clear plastic jars with holes in the top. You can use them to hold insects while you observe them. Carry a flashlight for peering into dark places. And don't forget your magnifying glass, a pen or pencil, and a journal or notebook.

# Tips for Explorers

Use your senses when you go exploring. Look around you. Do you see any animal tracks or holes in the ground or trees? Touch the bark of a tree trunk. Is it smooth or bumpy? Listen. Do you hear a rustle in the leaves? Or the chattering of a squirrel? Sniff the air. Can you smell a salty breeze from the ocean? Or the rotten-egg smell of a muddy pond? The more you pay attention to the world around you, the more of nature's secrets you'll discover.

To most of the animals you'll be looking at, you are big and scary. Move slowly and stay as quiet as possible so you don't scare them away.

To use your magnifying glass, first get close to the object or creature you want to look at. Then close one eye, and look through the other. Hold the magnifying glass up to your eye, then move it closer or farther away until you get a sharp view. If you're indoors, use a lamp for bright light.

When you're finished looking at an insect or other small creature with your magnifying glass, set it free. But use care—it may bite. If you turn over a rock or move a log, put it back. It's home to many creatures. Smell the flowers— don't pick them. Look at them through your magnifying glass, then draw what you see in your journal. Leave everything as you found it. Then it will be there for you to enjoy the next time you go exploring.

**FIGHT FIRES!**
Never focus your magnifying glass on paper or dry leaves in direct sunlight. You could start a fire.

# Taking Notes

Use a journal or notebook to take notes or draw pictures of everything you see. Something with blank pages is ideal, but lined paper is fine, too. Write down when and where you saw the animal or plant, and what the weather was like. If you're writing about an animal, note what it was doing when you saw it. Later, you can use these clues and a field guide to identify what you saw. Field guides contain pictures of the local plants and animals.

## Plant Clues

Look at the shape and color of leaves, buds, flowers, and seeds. Is the leaf shaped like an oval or a heart? Do some parts of it stick out farther than others? Are the edges smooth or are they jagged like the teeth of a saw? If it's fall, what color is it? Look at the flower. Some flowers, like the daisy, look like only one flower, but are really many flowers. Are the seeds round or flat? Do they have a "wing" on either side? Look for details with your magnifying glass.

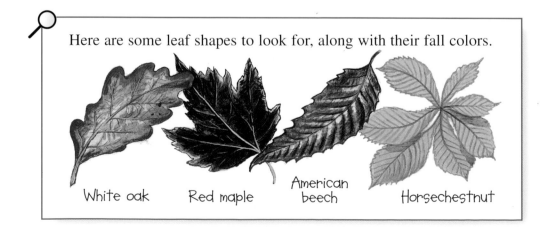

Here are some leaf shapes to look for, along with their fall colors.

White oak    Red maple    American beech    Horsechestnut

## Animal Clues

Look for tracks in soft dirt, mud, sand, or snow. If you find a feather, note its size, shape, and color. If you spot a strange bug, write down how big it is. Is it smaller than a quarter? Count its legs and body parts. Does it have wings? What color is it? Where did you see it? Did the animal make a noise? Can you describe it?

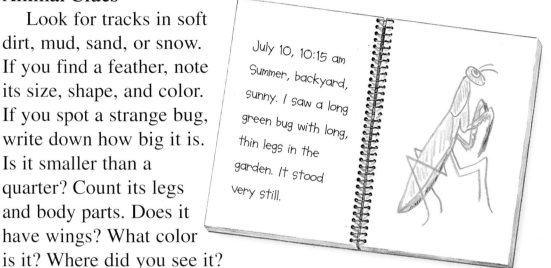

July 10, 10:15 am Summer, backyard, sunny. I saw a long green bug with long, thin legs in the garden. It stood very still.

Take a look at these creatures. They all belong to a group called arthropods. That means they all have an outer shell instead of an inner skeleton, and legs with joints. But they are not all insects. Can you see how they are different?

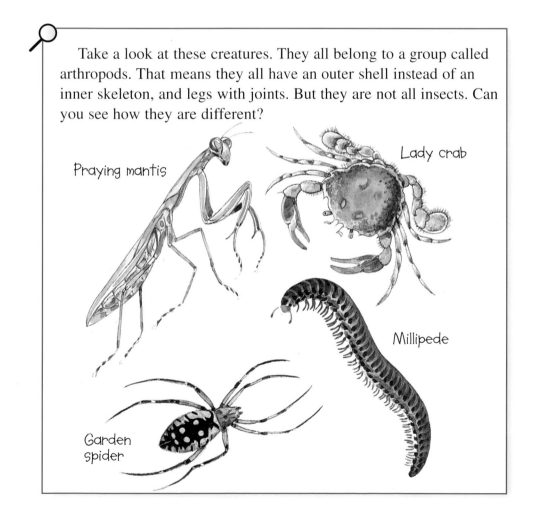

Praying mantis

Lady crab

Millipede

Garden spider

# Into the Woods

It's springtime in the forest! Flowers bloom and new leaves sprout on the trees. Birds build nests and lay eggs. Animals that sleep through the winter wake up. Insects buzz, hop, and crawl everywhere. Next time you go for a walk in the woods, use your magnifying glass to take a closer look.

Somewhere on this page is an insect that looks like a twig. Can you find it? Read about it on page 15.

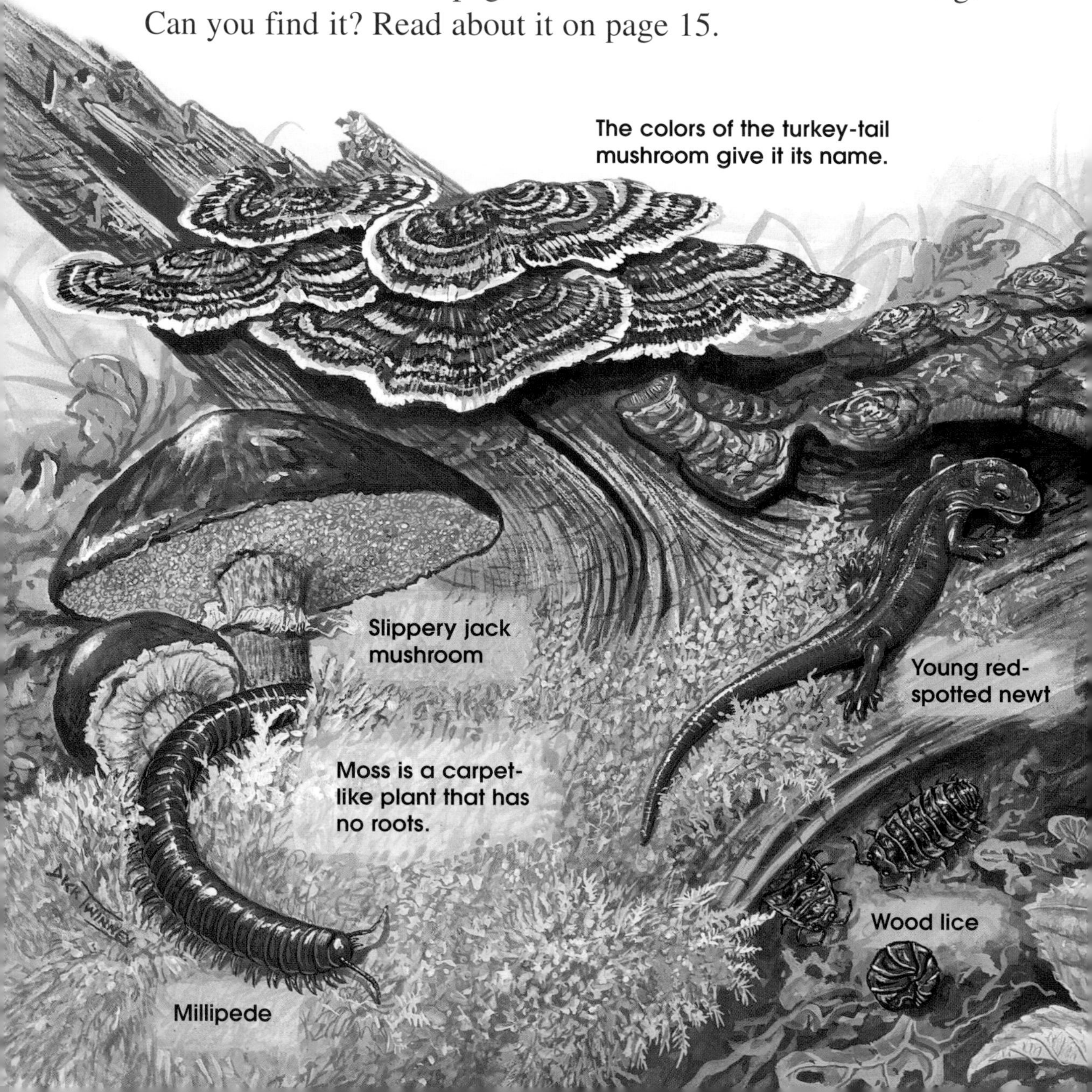

The colors of the turkey-tail mushroom give it its name.

Slippery jack mushroom

Moss is a carpet-like plant that has no roots.

Young red-spotted newt

Wood lice

Millipede

Lady fern

Trillium

The cap of the inky cap mushroom turns into a black liquid as it grows.

Click beetle

Slug

Trout lily

Violet

Lichen

After her eggs hatch, the forest wolf spider carries the spiderlings on her back.

Look closely at a rotting log and you'll discover a whole world you may not have noticed before. Everywhere you look, you'll see insects, spiders, and other small creatures. Look under the dead leaves on the forest floor. Can you find mushrooms growing? Or the tiny shoots of new plants? One thing you'll soon discover is that the more you look, the more you see.

## Slug

If you're out in the early morning, follow the slime trail of a slug. Slugs hide during the day and come out at night to feed on plants. They see and smell with their thick antennae.
Use your magnifying glass to look at a slug's back. Can you see its breathing hole?

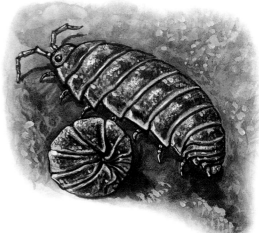

## Wood Louse

Turn over a rock and you'll probably find a wood louse. (You might know it as a pill bug or a sow bug.) If you gently touch this small creature, it will curl up into a ball to protect itself. Look through your magnifying glass to see how the parts of its hard shell fit together.

## Click Beetle

This insect is one of the acrobats of the bug world. When it's overturned, it snaps a peg on its belly to flip itself high into the air. The noise is loud enough to hear. With luck, the bug lands on its feet and scuttles away.

## Log Jam

Take a look under a rotting log and see what you can find.

### What You'll Need

A friend

2 pencils or pens

2 pieces of paper

### What to Do

1. Look for a dead log on the forest floor. Stand at one end and have your friend stand at the other. Have your pencils and paper ready.

2. Roll the log over. For safety's sake, be sure to keep the log between you and the creatures.

3. See how many creatures you can find and identify.

4. Write their names down. If you don't know a bug's name, draw it and see if you can find it in a field guide later.

5. Compare notes with your friend. Which one of you saw the most bugs? Did you see the same ones or different ones?

6. When you're finished, roll the log back into place

If you can't get to a forest, try this. Leave a flat board out on damp ground in your backyard overnight. In the morning, lift up the board and you will probably find slugs, beetles, and other creatures.

### Walkingstick

Did you find this strange-looking insect on page 13? This walkingstick is almost 4 inches (10 cm) long. Male walkingsticks are brown and females are greenish-brown. Their twig-like look helps to hide them from hungry birds.

## Creepy-Crawlies

How can you tell them all apart? Slugs have soft bodies and no legs. So do worms, but they have no antennae. Insects like ants and beetles have six legs and three parts to their bodies. Many of them have wings. Spiders have eight legs and two body sections. Millipedes have about 230 legs! Centipedes may have different numbers of legs, but never less than 30.

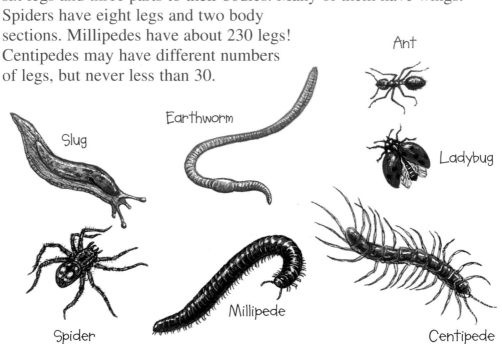

Ant

Earthworm

Slug

Ladybug

Spider

Millipede

Centipede

## Going Buggy!

"Bug" refers to lots of different creatures. Try this to practice noticing their differences.

### What You'll Need

4 or more small clear-plastic jars with lids

### What to Do

1. Collect as many different kinds of bugs as you can find. To do this without touching or hurting them, lay a jar on its side with the opening facing the animal. Let it crawl into the jar on its own.

2. Tip the jar up and loosely balance the lid on top to keep the bug inside.

3. Try counting the legs and body sections of each one. Use your magnifying glass. Can you tell whether the bugs you collected are insects or spiders? Millipedes or centipedes? Slugs or worms?

4. When you're done looking at the creatures, put them back where you found them.

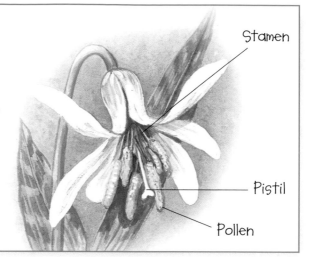

### FLOWER POWER

Look closely at the center of a wildflower with your magnifying glass. Right in the middle you should see the pistil, or female part of the flower. Around the pistil you'll see several stamens. These are the male parts of the flower that make pollen. Can you see the dustlike pollen at the ends?

Stamen

Pistil

Pollen

## Seedless Plants

Some plants don't produce flowers or seeds. Look under the cap of a slippery jack mushroom with your magnifying glass. Do you see the tiny holes? These holes produce spores, which will grow into new mushrooms. Now look under an inky cap mushroom. This mushroom's spores grow out of gills instead of holes.

## Lichen

Lichens are flat, rootless plants that grow on rocks and trees. They can be gray, green, red, or orange. Lichens use a kind of acid to dissolve a thin layer of tree bark or rock and turn it into soil.

Never eat a wild mushroom—it may be poisonous!

Take a close look with your magnifying glass. Can you see the new soil underneath the lichen?

# Field Day

A field is a grassy place that nobody mows. That means the wildlife can really go wild! Plants try to attract insects to spread their pollen to other plants. Butterflies flutter from flower to flower, sipping nectar. Bumblebees collect pollen. Aphids suck plant juices while ants protect them from enemies. And spiders try to catch them all with their webs.

One winged creature sounds like a hummingbird, but isn't one. Find it in this scene, then read about it on page 21.

Don't touch mayweed! It can irritate your skin.

Shamrock spider

Bumblebee

Ants

Aphids

Earthworm

Grasshopper

Viceroy butterfly

The honeybee does a "dance" to tell other bees where to find food.

Poison ivy

Queen Anne's lace

Daddy longlegs

Ladybug

Cricket

Milkweed

Milkweed tiger moth caterpillar

Monarch butterfly

The fiery searcher beetle is also known as the caterpillar hunter.

## A Field Up Close

To small creatures, a meadow is more like a towering forest. To a beetle, Queen Anne's lace is as tall as a tree and drops of rain can be a deadly disaster. On the other hand, a blade of grass can provide food, shelter from the elements and from enemies, and even a safe place to lay eggs.

### Shamrock Spider
If you go out early in the morning, you may see spider webs covered with dew. They probably belong to the shamrock spider. This spider spins a brand-new web every night. What happens to the old web? The spider eats it!

### Daddy Longlegs
Don't let this creature fool you. It may look like a spider, but it's not. The daddy longlegs has two eyes (true spiders have more) and appears to have one body section. It also can't spin silk. It belongs to a group of spider cousins called harvestmen.

### FLY AWAY HOME
When some baby spiders hatch, they spin a tiny thread of silk. Wind catches the silk and carries the spiderlings far away. Sometimes they drift as high as 3 miles (4.8 km) up in the air! The spiderling makes its home wherever the wind drops it off.

## Ladybug

A ladybug may eat 5,000 aphids in its lifetime! Can you tell how old a ladybug is by the number of spots it has? No. The spots only tell you what kind of ladybug it is. Some ladybugs have no spots at all!

## Ants and Aphids

Find an aphid on the stem of a plant or the back of a leaf. Take a hair from your head and stroke the aphid's abdomen. The insect will make a drop of honeydew. Ants love this sweet liquid and raise aphids to get it.

## Carried Away

An ant touches its body to the ground as it walks. This leaves a scent trail. Other ants can smell the trail with their feet! You can see this for yourself. Put a piece of candy several inches away from an anthill. Watch as one ant finds the food. How long does it take for the ant to make a trail that leads other ants to the candy?

### Hummingbird Moth

Did you find this moth on page 19? Like its namesake, the hummingbird moth whirs its wings as it hovers over flowers, sipping nectar. Look for the red and orange bands on its thick body and the clear spots on its wings.

## Monarch Butterfly

Monarch caterpillars eat milkweed leaves, which contain a poisonous milky-white juice. The poison doesn't hurt them. In fact, it helps them. Because of it, the monarch butterfly tastes bad and predators leave it alone.

## Viceroy Butterfly

This butterfly looks a lot like a monarch. Scientists used to think viceroys copied monarchs in order to fool predators into leaving them alone. But it turns out that viceroys taste bad, too.

## Butterfly or Moth?

Here are some ways to tell moths from butterflies. Moth antennae are straight or feathery. Butterflies have threadlike antennae that are thicker at the ends. Most moths rest with their wings out to the side. Butterflies rest with their wings straight up over their back. Butterflies are usually active in the daytime and moths at night.

Butterfly

Moth

---

### GROWING UP

Butterflies and moths start out as eggs. When they hatch, the larvae are better known as caterpillars. Caterpillars eat, eat, eat! Some caterpillars eat so much they kill plants. When the caterpillar is fully grown, it spins a chrysalis (butterfly) or cocoon (moth). Over time, the pupa inside turns into a butterfly or a moth.

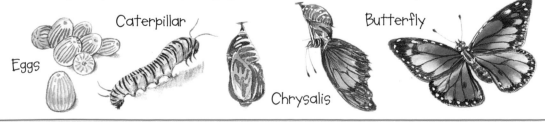

Eggs

Caterpillar

Chrysalis

Butterfly

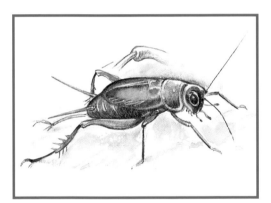

## A Mini Bouquet

Take a closer look at a daisy with your magnifying glass. The yellow center is actually made up of hundreds of tiny flowers! Each white petal is also a separate flower, called a ray flower. If you pull out one petal and take a peek with your magnifier, you will see the female part of the flower.

*Do not go near bees if you are allergic (or may be allergic) to bee venom!*

## Bumblebee

It's easy to tell the difference between honeybees and bumblebees—bumblebees are big, fat, and fuzzy! This fuzzy coat helps them to stay warm so they can fly in colder weather than most bees.

## Cricket

Male crickets "chirp" to attract a mate. To make this high-pitched sound, the cricket rubs its front wings together. Try this when you hear a cricket. Count how many chirps you hear in 15 seconds, then add 40 to that number. Your answer will be very close to the current temperature in degrees Fahrenheit! Why? The warmer it gets, the faster a cricket chirps.

### LEAVES OF THREE—LET THEM BE!

Poison ivy has shiny leaves that grow in groups of three. You may see poison ivy growing low to the ground. But it can also be a woody vine with hairy roots. Be very careful! If you think a plant is poison ivy, don't touch it. Poison ivy can irritate your skin and cause itching, swelling, and blisters.

# Still Waters

In summer, the pond is bursting with life. Everywhere you look, animals are flying, swimming, or crawling. And there are even more tiny animals that you can't see. One square inch (6.5 square cm) of pond mud can contain billions of bacteria.

One animal in this scene is known for his deep bellowing call. Can you spot him? Find out more on page 27.

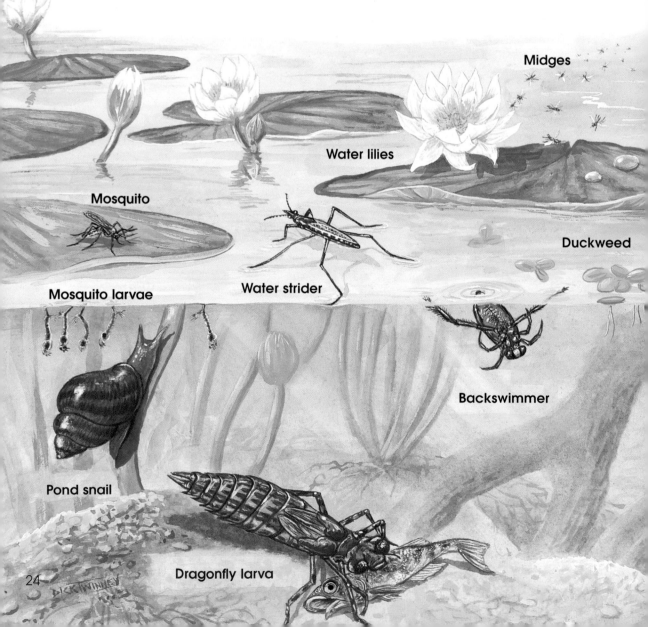

Midges

Water lilies

Mosquito

Duckweed

Mosquito larvae

Water strider

Backswimmer

Pond snail

Dragonfly larva

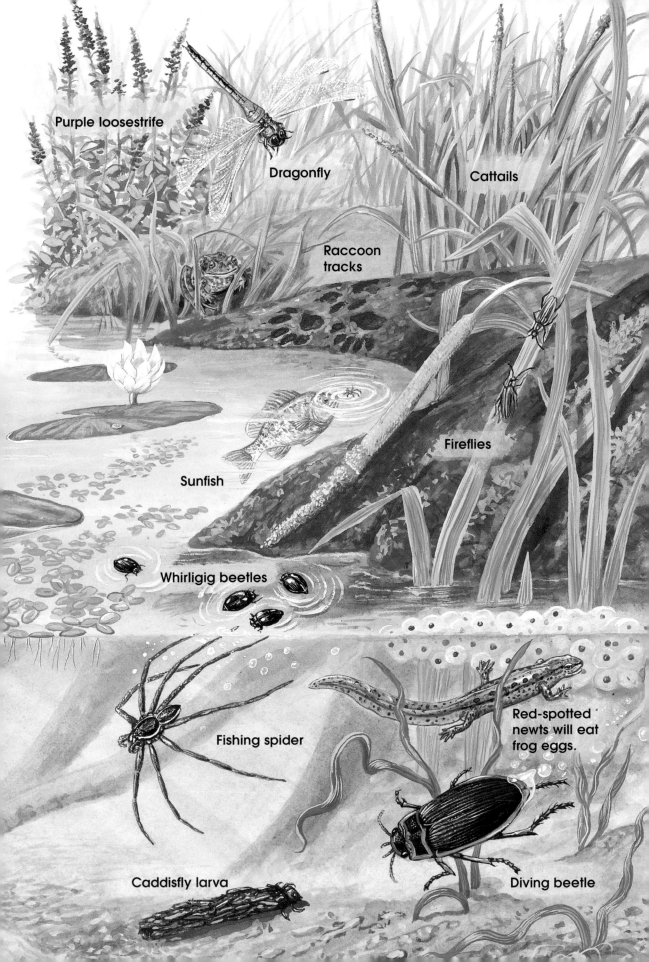

Purple loosestrife

Dragonfly

Cattails

Raccoon tracks

Fireflies

Sunfish

Whirligig beetles

Red-spotted newts will eat frog eggs.

Fishing spider

Caddisfly larva

Diving beetle

# A Pond Up Close

The warm, still water of a pond is a perfect breeding spot for all kinds of insects. You can see some of the young, or larvae. Wearing rubber gloves, scoop up some pond water in a clear-plastic jar. Use a sieve to scoop some mud from the shallows into a another jar. Let the water and mud settle. Use your magnifying glass to see how many animals you can find. Then return the water and mud to the pond.

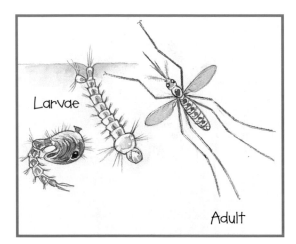

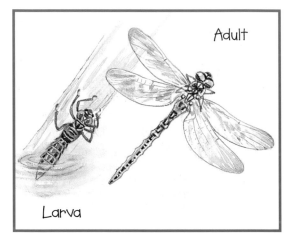

## Mosquito

When mosquito eggs hatch, the larvae float just under the surface of the water. They breathe through a tube that sticks up into the air. Only female adult mosquitoes feed on blood. They don't really bite, but pierce the skin with their needle-shaped mouthparts.

## Dragonfly

Dragonfly larvae live in water. They eat insects, tadpoles, and even small fish. The adult dragonfly is big and fast. It also has great vision. Each one of its two large eyes has 28,000 smaller eyes, or lenses. And each lens can see things separately!

## Caddisfly

The caddisfly larva hides itself in a case it builds from bits of leaves, stems, and stones. It holds the bits together with spit. If you find a caddisfly larva, you'll see its head poking out of the open end. Look at it with your magnifying glass. The mothlike adults come out at night.

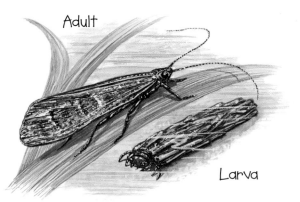

Larva

Adult

## Diving Beetle

The long, thin larvae of diving beetles are called water tigers. Why? Because they are such fierce hunters. The adult beetle uses its back legs like oars. It can trap air under its wing covers to stay underwater for a long time.

Adult

## Red-spotted Newt

When they are about four months old, the young newts grow lungs and leave the pond for the forest. After a few years, their color changes to green with red spots, and they return to the pond. Here they will mate and lay their own eggs.

## Underwater Up Close

You can make your own magnifying glass that will work underwater!

### What You'll Need

A large can (about the size of a coffee can)

Plastic wrap

2 or 3 strong rubber bands

### What to Do

1. Ask an adult to remove both ends of the can.

2. Stretch a large piece of plastic wrap across one end. The plastic should be as smooth as you can make it.

3. Use a few strong rubber bands to hold the plastic wrap in place.

4. When you go to the pond, push the can into the water, plastic side down. Look through the open end of the can to get a clear, close-up view of what's happening! Like a magnifying glass, light traveling through the water will slightly enlarge what you see.

### Bullfrog

Did you find this creature on page 25? The males are known for their "jug-o-rum" call. Bullfrogs are the largest frog in North America. Their back legs can grow up to 10 inches (25 cm) long. In winter, bullfrogs burrow into the mud at the bottom of the pond.

## It's a Frog's Life

Frogs begin their life as eggs. When they hatch, the young are called tadpoles. Tadpoles swim underwater and breathe through gills. Before long, the tadpoles begin to grow legs. Then they develop lungs to replace their gills. After they leave the water, their tails slowly disappear into their bodies.

Eggs

Adults

Newly hatched tadpole

Tadpole

Froglet

## Cattails

These tall plants grow up through the water from underground roots. The fruit, shaped like a cigar, contains hundreds of seeds. Many pond animals depend on cattails for food and shelter.

### Hatch Some Frog Eggs!

If you see a jelly-like blob of eggs at the edge of the water, chances are you've found frog eggs! Try hatching some yourself. Fill a jar with pond water. Scoop a few eggs into the jar. Keep the uncovered jar in a safe, shady spot. Look at the eggs with your magnifying glass. Can you see the tadpoles growing inside? As soon as the eggs hatch, return the tadpoles to the pond.

## Fishing Spider

Look for fishing spiders scuttling across rocks, plants, and the surface of the pond. These spiders can stay underwater for a half hour or more. They breathe air that has been trapped by their body hairs.

## Whirligig Beetle

These beetles swim around in circles on the surface of the water. Whirligig beetles have two-part eyes. They use the top half see above water and the bottom half to see underwater.

## Walking on Water

The water strider darts about on the surface of the water. How does it stay on top? Surface tension. The water molecules below pull on the surface molecules. This pull makes the surface water draw together into the smallest area it can. The same force is what makes water form droplets on the surface of a leaf. To see how surface tension works, try this.

### What You'll Need

Water glass

Water

Unused staple

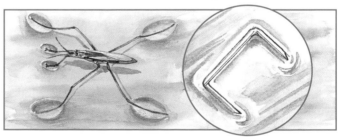

### What to Do

1. Fill the glass until the water is just even with the rim.
2. Hold the staple flat with the ends between your finger and thumb. Rest your thumb on the rim of the glass. Gently let go of the staple. Does it float? If not, try it again.
3. Use your magnifying glass to look at the water around the staple. Can you see the water bulging slightly around the staple? That's caused by surface tension!

# On the Beach

If you've ever gone to the seashore, you've probably picked up a few empty shells to take home. Have you wondered about the creatures that once lived in them? You can find out about some of them in the next few pages. Then next time you visit the beach, take a closer look with your magnifying glass.

Look for a strange-looking eight-legged creature peering out from its burrow. Then turn to page 27 to read about it.

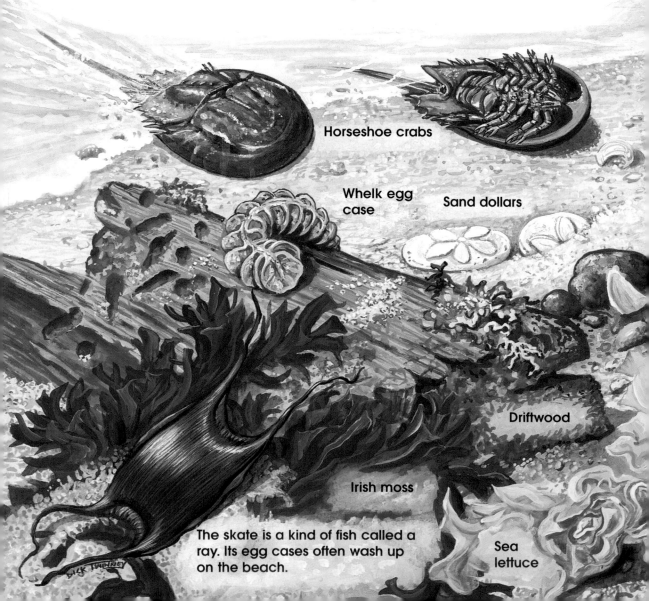

Horseshoe crabs

Whelk egg case

Sand dollars

Driftwood

Irish moss

The skate is a kind of fish called a ray. Its egg cases often wash up on the beach.

Sea lettuce

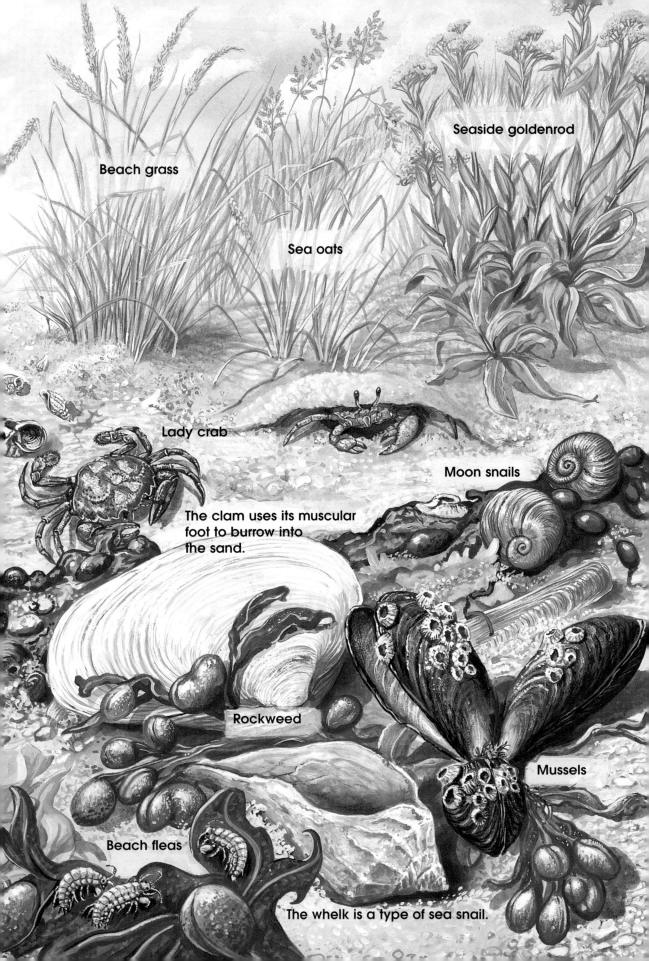

Seaside goldenrod

Beach grass

Sea oats

Lady crab

Moon snails

The clam uses its muscular foot to burrow into the sand.

Rockweed

Mussels

Beach fleas

The whelk is a type of sea snail.

On your next visit to the beach, explore the washed-up shells, seaweed, and driftwood left at the high-tide line. Some of the things may have been carried for hundreds of miles by the ocean. Use your magnifying glass to look at them. Draw them in your journal. Later, look in a field guide and see if you can identify what you found.

## Beach Fleas

These small creatures are not really fleas, but they hop about like them. Beach fleas eat decaying seaweed and dead animals. They usually spend the day in their burrows. But you may spot a few if you look closely at the high-tide line.

### BITS AND PIECES

Pick up a handful of sand. Look at it with your magnifying glass. What do you see? Sand is made up of rock, shells, and coral that have been worn down into tiny pieces by the movement of the ocean.

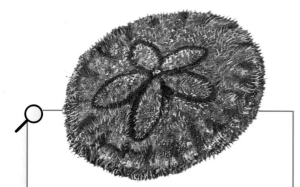

### SAND DOLLAR

See if you can find the flat, round shell of a sand dollar. Use your magnifying glass to look at the flower shape on the top. When the sand dollar was alive (see above), it breathed through tiny tube feet that came out of the slits.

## Horseshoe Crab

Horseshoe crabs spend the winter buried in mud on the bottom of the Atlantic Ocean. But in spring, they head for shore, where the females lay their eggs. As they grow, horseshoe crabs shed their shells. Look for one on the beach.

## Mussels

The beards of mussels are really the fine threads the mussel uses to anchor itself to rock or other solid objects. If you find an empty mussel shell on the beach, see if it still has any of the threads attached. Look at them through your magnifying glass.

*Check out the wide bands on the outside of a mussel shell. Each one stands for a year's growth. Count them to find out the age of the mussel.*

## Barnacles

These small animals glue themselves headfirst to solid objects. You may see them on rock, dock pilings, boat bottoms—even other sea animals. To eat, barnacles open the plates at the top of their shell. Then they wave their feathery legs around in the water to scoop up tiny bits of food.

### PLANKTON

Mussels, barnacles, and many other creatures begin their lives as plankton. Plankton is made up of millions of tiny animals and plants that drift in the ocean. It's eaten by many kinds of animals, from the largest blue whale to—well—mussels and barnacles.

## Light as a Feather

Look for a feather on the beach. Separate some of the strands. Look at them through your magnifying glass. Can you see the tiny hairlike hooks on the strands? You've found a flight feather. Now stroke the strands between your fingers. See how the hooks reattach? A bird preens, or smoothes its feathers, by stroking them with its beak.

### Ghost Crab

Did you find this animal on page 31? The ghost crab has gills and can't breathe air, but it spends most of its time on land. How? It carries seawater inside its body. At night, the ghost crab comes out of its burrow to get a fresh supply of seawater and to hunt beach fleas and other food.

# Tide Pools

Tide pools are small bodies of seawater left behind in the rocks when the tide goes out. Look for them on the rocky shorelines of New England and along the West Coast. Tide pools are fascinating to look at, but if you visit one, be careful. Stay close to shore, and only explore while the tide is out.

**DO NOT DISTURB!**
Never remove living creatures from the tide pool.

## Hermit Crab

Do you see a shell moving quickly along the bottom, propelled by legs? You've found a hermit crab! These crabs have no shell of their own. To protect their soft bodies, they move into the empty shells of other creatures.

## Sea Star

Sea stars eat mussels, snails, and other sea creatures. To eat, the sea star moves its body over the closed shell. It uses its arms to slowly pull on the shell until it opens just a little bit. Then the sea star pushes it stomach through its mouth, and into the shell! After digesting the soft animal inside, it pulls its stomach back into itself.

**ALL CUT UP**
What happens if a sea star is cut into pieces? Each part that has a bit of the center section will grow into a complete new sea star!

Sea lettuce

Sea urchins

Sea star

## Sea Urchin

These algae-eating animals look like pincushions. Don't touch! Most will not harm you, but some have sharp spines that may cut you. When the animal dies, the spines fall off. Then only the hard outer shell, called a test, remains.

## Sea Anemone

These plant look-alikes are really animals. They wait for prey to come to them. When a passing fish brushes against it, an anemone shoots stinging threads from its tentacles. The threads paralyze the fish. Then the anemone draws the prey into its mouth.

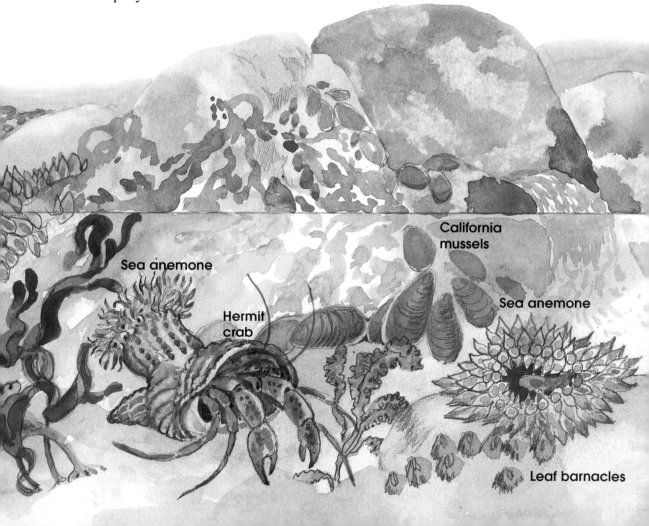

California mussels

Sea anemone

Sea anemone

Hermit crab

Leaf barnacles

# Your Own Backyard

In most parts of North America, the weather starts to cool off in the fall. Many leaves begin to change color and plants go to seed. Squirrels are busy storing nuts. And overhead, many birds are flying south for the winter. There's no better place to watch these changes than in your own backyard.

Some people think one animal in this picture can predict the weather. Can you find it? Read more about it on page 39.

Red clover

Chrysalis

Sugar maple

Little black ants live in underground colonies, where they spend the winter.

Black oak

Blow on the fluffy white globe
of a late season dandelion
and watch the seeds scatter.

Take care! The
outer shell of the
horsechestnut
has sharp spikes.

Pinecone

Cicada skin

House fly

Earthworm

Acorns

Jumping spider

White oak

DICK TWINNEY

The leaves of many trees change color in the fall. Why? Because they stop making chlorophyll. Chlorophyll gives leaves their green color. It also helps soak up the sunlight needed to make food. When there is less chlorophyll, the leaves turn color. They also stop making food and begin to die. Trees that lose their leaves in the fall are called decidous.

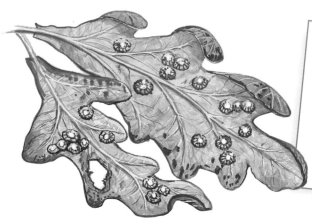

## BUMPY LEAVES

Look at different leaves with your magnifying glass. Do any of the leaves have bumps? These may be galls. A gall forms when an insect lays its egg inside the leaf.

## Turning Red

Many fall leaves turn yellow. But some trees, like red maples and black oaks, turn red. Besides warm days and cool nights, the leaves on these trees need direct sunlight to turn red. Try this experiment and see what happens.

### What You'll Need

Masking tape

### What to Do

1. Before the leaves change color, find a red maple or another tree that you know turns red in the fall. Look for one with low branches that you can reach.

2. Put a piece of masking tape on the top of a few leaves that get direct sunlight.

3. After the leaves change color, remove the tape. What color is the area that was under the tape?

## Cicada

These noisy insects make the loud, sharp buzzing noise you hear on hot summer days. As cicadas grow, they shed their hard outer skins. See if you can find a leftover skin hanging from a branch or a tree trunk.

## Jumping Spider

Excellent hunters, jumping spiders stalk their prey. When they get close enough, they raise their front legs and—pounce! These small spiders can jump more than 10 times the length of their own body.

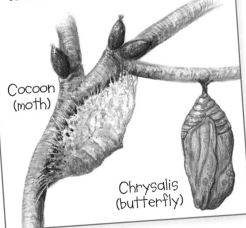

### ALL WRAPPED UP

A chrysalis has a metallic sheen and will be attached to a twig at one or more points. A cocoon looks dry and papery. It may be wrapped in a leaf or attached to a twig all along its length. If you find a cocoon or a chrysalis, look at it through your magnifying glass. Check on it through the winter. In the spring, watch for the butterfly or moth to come out!

Cocoon
(moth)

Chrysalis
(butterfly)

## Red Clover

Most clover leaves have three lobes, but some have four. Finding a four-leaf clover is considered by some people to be good luck. The flowers of some red clovers bloom through the first frost of winter.

### Woolly Bear Caterpillar

Did you find this bristly black-and-red larva of the Isabella moth on page 37? There are people who say that the thicker the black ends, the worse the coming winter will be. What does it really tell you? How close the caterpillar is to being fully grown.

## Seed Roundup

Seeds come in all shapes and sizes. See how many different kinds you can find in your yard or garden. Don't forget that nuts are seeds, too. Before you can look at the seeds inside, you may need to break the fruit or the seed pod open. Use your magnifying glass to get a closer look.

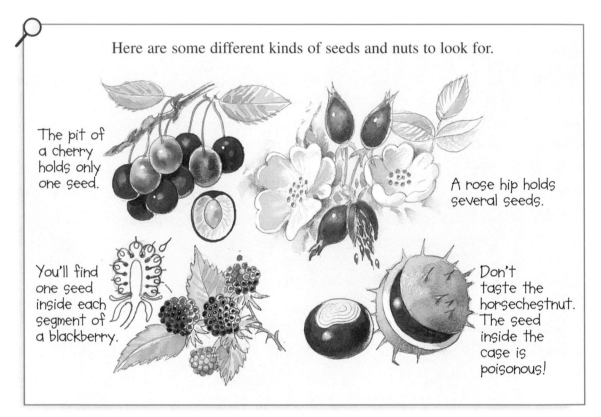

Here are some different kinds of seeds and nuts to look for.

The pit of a cherry holds only one seed.

A rose hip holds several seeds.

You'll find one seed inside each segment of a blackberry.

Don't taste the horsechestnut. The seed inside the case is poisonous!

### Growing Acorns

Try sprouting a few acorns. Put some pebbles in a shallow soup bowl and fill it with water. Add a few acorns. Make sure the bottom of each acorn is partly in the water. Add more water as needed. In a few weeks, a thick white root will crack open the bottom of the acorns. Soon a small stem will sprout from the other end, and tiny leaves will grow. Look at your baby oak trees with your magnifying glass.

## Earthworm

Earthworms don't have eyes, but they can sense light through their skin. They also breathe through it! Why do you see more earthworms after it's rained? When it rains, the spaces between clumps of dirt fill up with water. If the earthworm doesn't come to the surface, it will drown.

## Wonder Worms

Earthworms eat dead plants, which they soon turn into rich soil. Look for the little mounds of castings that a worm leaves at the edge of its hole. As earthworms burrow through the dirt, they loosen it up. This helps air and water to pass through it more easily. Try collecting some worms and watch what they do.

### What You'll Need

Cornmeal

Large jar

Soil from the yard

Sand

Potting soil

Water

Earthworms

Lettuce

Paper

### What to Do

1. Pour some cornmeal into the jar.
2. Add a layer of soil from your yard, then add sand and potting soil.
3. Sprinkle water over the top.
4. Carefully collect a few earthworms and put them in the jar.
5. Put the jar in a dark place. How long does it take for the worms to reach the bottom? Do they stir up the layers of dirt and sand? Leave a piece of lettuce on top of the soil for the worms to eat.
6. Look at one of the worms with your magnifying glass. Can you see tiny hairs running along one side? These are called setae, and they help the worm move. Put the worm on a piece of paper to hear the setae scratch. When you are done, put the worms back outside.

## Out in the Cold

You may not think so, but even in cold weather, there's a lot to see with your magnifying glass. Try getting a closer look at snowflakes before they melt to see how different they really are. Or take a look at the buds on bushes and trees in the late winter.

### Watch it, Bud!

In the winter, trees and bushes may look lifeless without their leaves, but they're not! Get out your magnifying glass and take a closer look. Can you see the tiny buds waiting to open in the spring? Some buds will become flowers. Others will become leaves.

### This Place Is Jumping

Go for a walk on a warm winter day and you might see a dark patch on the snow. The patch is really made of tiny, jumping creatures called snow fleas. Look at them through your magnifying glass. Snow fleas aren't really fleas, but a kind of insect called springtails.

White pine

### Pine or Spruce?

Pines have bunches of 2 to 5 needlelike leaves growing from one spot. The needles of spruce and fir trees don't grow in bunches. Each one grows from a separate spot on the branch.

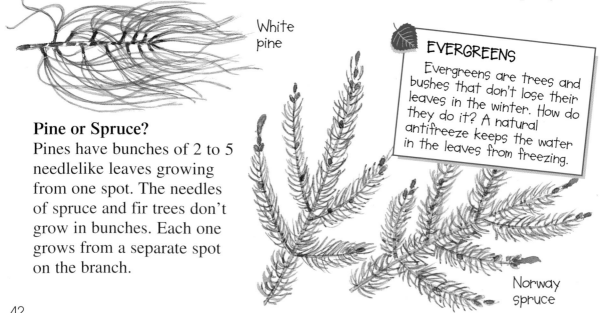

### EVERGREENS

Evergreens are trees and bushes that don't lose their leaves in the winter. How do they do it? A natural antifreeze keeps the water in the leaves from freezing.

Norway spruce

Needle | Column | Plate | Star

## Singular Sensation

Snowflakes are really bunches of tiny ice crystals that are stuck together. Depending on the air temperature and humidity, snowflakes form in flat plates or in long needles. Snowflakes are always six-sided, and no two are ever alike.

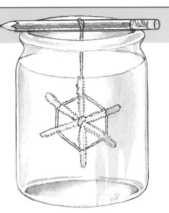

You can grow your own snowflake in a jar! It will last a lot longer than the real thing and will be just as sparkly.

### What You'll Need

White pipe cleaner    Wide-mouth jar
String    Boiling water
Pencil    Borax powder

### What to Do

1. Cut a pipe cleaner into three equal sections. Twist them together in the center to make a star.

2. Moving clockwise, wrap the string around each of the pipe cleaner sections to form a snowflake shape.

3. Tie one end of a piece of string to the snowflake. Tie the other end to a pencil.

4. Ask an adult to help with this part. Fill the jar with boiling water. Add three tablespoons of borax and stir after each one.

5. Lower the snowflake into the jar. Let the pencil rest on top of the jar to hold the snowflake in place overnight. The snowflake shouldn't touch the bottom of the jar.

6. The next morning, remove the snowflake. It will be covered in shiny crystals.

Don't forget to use your magnifier to get a good, close-up look at the crystals. Are they large or small? How many sides do they have?

# Glossary

**antennae:** The sense organs on an animal's head that allow it to smell, touch, or hear.

**arthropod:** An animal that has jointed legs and a body with more than one section. The body has an outer shell instead of an inner skeleton. Insects, spiders, and millipedes are all arthropods.

**bug:** A word that is often used for many kinds of small creatures, such as insects, spiders, snails, and millipedes. It's also the name of one large group of insects that have certain things in common.

**caterpillar:** The larval or young stage of a butterfly or moth.

**chlorophyll:** The material found in plants that is used to make food. It also gives plants their green color.

**chrysalis:** A covering made by butterfly caterpillars that hides and protects them while they turn into adults.

**cocoon:** A covering made by moth caterpillars that hides and protects them while they turn into adults.

**field:** An area of land that contains mostly uncut grasses.

**field guide:** A book with facts and pictures that is used to identify different kinds of animals, plants, rocks, shells, and other things in nature.

**gills:** The body parts that let animals breathe underwater. Some mushrooms have plates beneath their caps called gills where spores are produced.

**habitat:** The area in nature where a kind of plant or animal grows or lives.

**insect:** An arthropod with three body sections, six jointed legs, antennae, and an outer shell instead of an inner skeleton.

**larva:** The young stage of insects. Many insects hatch from eggs into larvae that look completely different from their adult forms.

**lichen:** Flat, rootless plants that can grow on surfaces like rocks and tree trunks.

**magnifying glass:** A piece of curved glass that you can look through to see an enlarged view of plants and animals.

**mushroom:** A kind of plant that produces spores instead of seeds. It has no chlorophyll. Because of this, many scientists put mushrooms in a separate group from plants. This group is called fungi.

**nectar:** A sugary liquid made by flowering plants.

**pistil:** The female part of a flower. When pollen comes into contact with the pistil, seeds are produced.

**plankton:** The many kinds of tiny creatures, plants, and animal eggs that float in fresh or salt water.

**pollen:** The tiny, dustlike grains on the stamen of a plant. When pollen comes into contact with the pistil, seeds are produced.

**predator:** An animal that hunts and eats other animals.

**prey:** Animals that are eaten by other animals or plants.

**pupa:** The last stage of an insect before it turns into an adult. At this stage, the insect usually goes into hiding to complete the changes that make it an adult.

**seed:** The fertilized egg of a plant. It will produce a new plant when it grows.

**setae:** Tiny hairs on an earthworm's body that help it move.

**spider:** An eight-legged arthropod with two body parts. It can spin silk.

**spore:** What a mushroom produces instead of a seed that can grow into a new mushroom.

**stamen:** The male part of a plant that produces pollen.

**tadpole:** The young stage of a frog. Like insects, frogs go through different stages of development before they become adults.

# Index

*To see a world in a grain of sand*
*And a heaven in a wild flower,*
*Hold infinity in the palm of your hand*
*And eternity in an hour*

—*William Blake*